A HOMAGE TO DIVINITY

SRI THAKUR SATYANANDA IN DEVOTEE'S EYE - VOLUME 1

DEBANJAN ROY

Dedicated to the sacred memory of my Baba (Father) Late Debi Prosad Roy, and Maa (Mother) Late Shubhra Roy.

None of them is now on this earth in their physical forms. But I have the strongest faith that they are always with me and guiding me at every moment of my life.

So, it is an honour to submit my offering at their lotus feet and seek their blessings.

Contents

Contents

Prayers

God is our Divine Mother, Maa.

Maa, we are Your children. Please hold our hands at all times and lead us on the path of righteousness. And kindly bless this humble effort to offer our homage to Sri Thakur.

With Your blessings, the Divine Journey Begins...

Acknowledgements

To make this book possible, I am ever grateful to my Guru, Her Holiness (late) Sri Archana Puri Maa of Sree Satyananda Devayatan, Kolkata.

Her Holiness had graced my life through the sacred 'Mantra Deeksha' (Spiritual Initiation) in 2006. Her blessings have been the continual source of my inspiration ever since I took up the pen and began writing.

Pranam at the lotus feet of my Guru!

Divinity Personified: Sri Thakur Satyananda

Sri Thakur Satyananda is the 'Avatar', the Human Reincarnation of the Supreme Godhead, who had graced this modern age.

He chose to appear in the devotion-filled household of Sri Mahendra Nath Mukhopadhyay and Smt Kashiswari Devi, as their second son, Satyabrata in February 1902 in Calcutta. And the miraculous incidents that occurred both before and after his divine birth indicated that God himself had made His descent onto the earth in the form of an 'Avatar'.

Intense spirituality was the hallmark of the illustrious life of Satyabrata throughout as he transitioned from his childhood to youth. His innate inclination towards a life of renunciation got a further boost through receipt of formal 'Mantra Deeksha (spiritual initiation) from His Holiness, Swami Abhedananda - a direct disciple of Bhagavan Ramakrishna Dev. After practising intense 'sadhana' (spiritual penance) at his own house for a prolonged period, Satyabrata was blessed by the Divine Mother Herself, who granted him the sacred vow of 'Sanyas' (monkhood) with a new monastic name, Satyananda.

Sri Satyananda continued his 'sadhana' at his ancestral house in Suri town in the Birbhum district of undivided Bengal. Gradually spiritual seekers started coming here to seek his holy company and ultimately in 1939, "Sri Ramakrishna Ashram" came to be formally opened at this very house. This was his first Ashram.

Over the next few years, many devotees took shelter under him and a dedicated group of monastic disciples chose to surrender themselves at his lotus feet for their whole life. And this God Incarnate came to be known as 'Sri Thakur Satyananda' among all.

Soon more branch Ashrams came up in various towns and villages of Bengal and Bihar. The Ashram located at Baranagar (on the outskirts of Calcutta) was the main one. Under the divine inspiration of Sri Thakur, each of these Ashrams became the hub for imparting Religion and Spirituality among the masses. Philanthropy - rendering humanitarian service to God in the form of the needy- was another important function here.

Next, and perhaps the most unique role of these Ashrams was spreading Divine art and culture among the general public. The array of channels employed by Sri Thakur for this noble aim was amazingly diverse: music, literature, dance, drama, sports, and many more.

And, perhaps, the most important contribution of each of these Spiritual centres was sowing the seeds of man-making education in children, the future citizens of this country, through schools and other educational institutions.

Sri Thakur's sacred 'Leela' (the holy life of a God Incarnate) continued for over three decades, during which the lives of innumerable devotees and followers got blessed by receiving the sacred spiritual initiation from him. And then in August 1969, Sri Thakur chose to cast off his mortal coils at his Baranagar Ashram. But that was just the end of his perishable body.

In his Divine form, Sri Thakur is always there with us, ever ready to shower his infinite grace upon all the earnest followers walking on the path of spirituality. So, I invite all of you to accompany me, as we seek to delve into the sacred life of Sri Thakur in the following pages and thus offer our homage at his lotus feet.

Pearls Of Divinity

The fragrance of divinity of a God-Incarnate always gets captured in his holy sayings. Therefore, such sayings are no less valuable than pearls.

A few such Divine pearls uttered by Sri Thakur are given below. Imbibing their essence will assuredly elevate our lives: -

- Be as pure as a flower.
- Holiness is the formula for this age. When you attain holiness, everything becomes possible.
- The essence of faith in God lies in surrendering to Him.
- Go on performing your duty while constantly praying to God and repeating His Holy Name.
- The way is faith - faith in the grace of God.
- Keep moving forward by keeping faith on one particular path.
- Keep on persevering towards your goal with strong faith.
- To be virtuous requires a 'strong will to be good' as its foundation.
- Ensure that you always keep repeating the Holy Name of God within your mind.
- Always keep your mind attuned towards the higher plane - be it in the spiritual matter or be it in the worldly affair.
- Always remember God is keeping watch over you - He is guiding you - keep this ever in mind.
- Through the habit of constant remembrance of God, we can create new channels of devotion in our brains.
- Just go on repeating the Holy Name of God - just go on

praying to Him - He will make everything alright.

- Holy Name of God is the only way in the present age.
- The essence of faith in God lies in surrendering to Him.
- 'Shraddha' is the main thing in life - it is 'shraddha' that propels a man forward in his life.

A Few Words Of Homage

The prime objective of writing this book is to offer my respect at the lotus feet of Sri Thakur Satyananda. In the sacred ‘Guru Parampara’ (Guru Tradition), he is my most revered ‘Param Guru’ - he is the Guru of Sri Archana Puri Maa and I am her blessed disciple.

The material for this volume has been primarily sourced from the authoritative texts on the sacred life of Sri Thakur, as penned by Swami Nirvedananda ji, Sri Archana Puri Maa, Sri Sadhana Puri Maa, and others. And then I have humbly tried to add my perspective as a devotee, based on my long association with Sri Satyananda order of monkhood since 2006.

Such a spiritual connection led to my long-felt urge to offer tribute to Sri Thakur through the medium of words. The present volume is an outcome of this inspiration. Here I have sought to depict just the bird’s eye view of the exceptional life of Sri Thakur.

I thank everyone who has encouraged me on this divine journey.

“Holy Name of God is the only way in the present age.”
- Sri Thakur

Glossary Of Terms Used

Many Sanskrit terms of 'Sanatan Dharma' have been used in this book. Their nearest equivalent English meanings are placed below:

Avatar: Incarnation of God in human form
Ashram: Monastery
Arati: A part of ritualistic worship of God
Amrit: Ambrosia
Bhagavan: God
Brahma: Absolute consciousness
Brahmacharya: Vow of celibacy
Baul: Folk music of Bengal
Dharma: Righteous way of life
Dhyana: Meditation on God
Dwitiya: Second day in a lunar month
Ekadashi: The eleventh day in a lunar fortnight
Guru: Spiritual preceptor
Gopal ji: Childhood form of Bhagavan Sri Krishna
Homa: Sacrifice to God present as the fire element
Japa: Repetition of Holy Name of God
Krishna: Dark fortnight in a lunar month
Kirtan: Devotional Music
Leela: Divine life and deeds of an Avatar
Maa: God as Divine Mother of cosmos
Mudra: Specific Step of Dance
Nirakar: Formless
Narayan: Part of Trinity of God in Sanatan Dharma
Param Guru: Guru of Guru
Puja: Worship of God
Pranam: Homage
Prasad: Consecrated food-offering to God

Phalgun: Month of spring in the lunar almanac
Sadhana: Spiritual endeavours to attain God
Samadhi: Union with the absolute consciousness
Shishya: Disciple
Sanyasi: Monk
Sanyasini: Nun
Sanyas: Renunciation of worldly life
Sanskar: Impressions of countless previous lives
Shishu: Child
Sammelan: Conference
Shraddha: Reverence
Sansar: Worldly life
Sudhi: Learned scholars
Sanatan: Eternal
Tithi: Date
Treta, Dwapar, Kali: Names of Yuga
Tabla: Percussion instrument of Indian Music
Tapasya: Spiritual austerity
Yogi: Ascetic
Yuga: Cyclic epoch in Cosmology of 'Sanatan Dharma', with each cycle lasting for 43,20,000 years

"God is always there with you - remember this." - Sri Thakur

Part 1

Sri Thakur's Sacred Life: A Glimpse

CHAPTER ONE

The Concept of Avatar

Friends, as all our scriptures and sages have declared repeatedly, God Supreme is the sole entity in the entire cosmos: everything in this universe is nothing but an image of God. This is true for man as well – a human being is 'Divinity' personified at his core...his very essence is purity.

But alas! Man, at times, is found to indulge in sin also - this happens under the unholy provocation of 'sanskar', the impression from the accumulated actions of all his previous lives. As a result, the earth starts getting filled with the polluting vibrations of gross sensuousness. And when such moral degeneration crosses its limits, the earth and its suffering humanity start desperately crying out for redemption.

Taking pity, God then descends into human form and gradually cleanses the earth of all its accumulated filth. This is the phenomenon of the Incarnation of God. In our 'Sanatan Dharma', such a Divinely merciful human form is called 'Avatar'. This blissful phenomenon has graced humanity multiple times in every single age.

Thus, Bhagavan Sri Rama Chandra descended in the 'Treta yuga' and brought 'Dharma' back to this thirsty world. And thereafter, our earth was blessed by the Divine aura of Bhagavan Sri Krishna in the 'Dwapar yuga' and this world was again got rid of corruption, leading to the re-establishment of 'Dharma'.

This Divine tradition of periodic descent of Godliness continued in the 'Kali yuga', with the births of Sri Buddha Dev, Sri Chaitanya Mahaprabhu, and then very recently, Bhagavan Ramakrishna Dev.

Sri Thakur Satyananda is the latest 'Avatar' in this Divine sequence to have blessed this earth in our modern age. And given the wanton darkness of this age, he is the perfect 'Avatar' for bringing back righteousness and restoring hope among his children.

In Srimad Bhagwat Gita, the holy scripture of 'Sanatan Dharma', God has promised to incarnate Himself, again and again, to re-establish the might of 'Dharma' on this earth and eliminate all the forces of darkness therefrom. Sri Thakur Satyananda's Divine incarnation took place under this noble pledge.

With this short introduction to 'Avatar' as the backdrop, let us now turn our attention to the sacred 'Leela' of Sri Thakur ... we begin by recapitulating the miraculous events surrounding His Divine birth.

"Self-knowledge, self-control and pin-point focus is the need of the hour." - Sri Thakur

CHAPTER TWO

The Divine Appearance of Avatar on Earth

Friends, come, let us offer our homage to Sri Thakur through a peek into the wonderful account of his Divine birth...

In accordance with the Divine roots of 'Avatar', each and every attribute connected with His life - his birth, his growing up, his human appearance, his actions, his sayings, and so on - has an element of the extraordinary built into it!

And, as we look into the Divine birth of Sri Thakur, this assertion is found to be very much true. For this episode of Reincarnation, God chose Sri Mahendra Nath and Smt Kashishwari Devi, to be the fortunate parents. Now, for a long time, this Divine couple had remained childless - their first two issues had been stillborn - this had remained a continual source of anguish for them. The same agony had tormented Kumud Kamini Devi (the pious mother of Mahendra Nath) too. Her long-cherished desire for a grandson had remained unfulfilled.

Hence, in desperation, she and her daughter-in-law decided to seek the assistance of Vilayet Ali (a well-known 'Fakir' - Muslim monk -belonging to the Birbhum district in

Bengal). The monk listened in sympathy to their sorrowful outpouring and assured them their longing for child-birth in the family was going to be fulfilled at last. Then, he called aside Kashishwari Devi and instructed her as follows: "O mother! You'll have to carry out a difficult form of 'Sadhana' in a cremation ground. And if you succeed in satisfactorily performing it, you can rest assured of giving birth to several children in succession. Among them, your second child is destined to grow up into one of the Greatest Saints to have ever blessed this Earth." She immediately committed to Vilayet Ali that she would carry out all his instructions to the T.

Accordingly, both the ladies set out for cremation ground in the dark hours of the night of an auspicious date indicated by Vilayet Ali. While Kumud Kamini Devi stopped at its periphery, her daughter-in-law fearlessly entered the solemn crematorium, sat down near a funeral pyre and performed the 'Sadhana', step by step, as per the precise instruction of Vilayet Ali. At its conclusion, both the ladies came back home, brimming with full faith that the predictions of the monk would certainly turn out to be true. In due course of time, their faith was amply rewarded when Kashishwari Devi gave birth to a son, much to the joy of the entire household.

Two years after this happy event, she was blessed with a uniquely Divine experience - it was a holy precursor of the imminent descent of God into human form! It so happened that Kashishwari Devi was lying down one night at her home in Kolkata - her mother-in-law was also sleeping beside her. All of a sudden, she was startled to discover a wonderful ray of illumination falling upon her body, while the rest of the room was covered in the darkness of night. In that dimness, she could just perceive that it was coming out of the holy worship room, located in front of her own bedroom.

Puzzled by this unusual spectacle, she woke up Kumud Kamini Devi, who initially thought that, someone on the road outside must have been sending that ray of light inside their room from his torch. However, her visit to the worship room was enough to dispel that impression. There she witnessed the magical sight of a Divine ray of light emanating from the holy icon of Bhagavan Narayan, the presiding deity of the household, whose Image was enshrined on the sacred throne in the worship room of the house. It was this light, travelling in the form of a ray, which was then falling upon the supine form of her daughter-in-law.

On beholding this scene, she was filled with the deepest reverence - this Divine marvel gave her a clear indication that Bhagavan Narayan Himself would be getting incarnated in human form in her own household soon! The prediction of the monk was about to come true - it was going to be the rarest of the rare blessings for the whole of humanity - and thus, she felt truly blessed at that moment!

Many Divine happenings continued to sanctify her devout household. For example, one day Kumud Kamini Devi was a fortunate witness to the sacred sight of four Godly children, the eternal companions of Sri Gopal ji, dancing around her daughter-in-law!

Likewise, both Mahendra Nath and Kashishwari Devi were favoured with holy visions too. The former got blessed with the Divine spectacle of Sri Gopal ji sitting on the lap of Mother Goddess Durga! And the latter got cheered with the dream of a Godly child, handsome in appearance and wearing lovely anklets on his feet, roaming hither and thither in her room!

And the much-awaited day arrived at last! It was the season of Spring and as per the lunar almanac, it was the month of Falgun. And this earth got glorified with the Divine appearance of 'Avatar' of Supreme Godhead, with the birth of the second son of Kashishwari Devi on the sacred 'Falgun - Krishna -Dwitiya tithi' (second day of the dark fortnight in the month of Falgun) at the City of Kolkata (then, Calcutta). As per the English calendar, it was the month of February 1902.

At birth, the infant looked as magnificent as the luminous rays of brilliant moonlight. However, to the worry of everyone, the baby did not start crying after his birth as expected - he continued to remain completely silent. So, the attending nurse frantically examined the new-born to make sure that he was alive. And it was a great relief to discover that everything was alright - only the eyes of the infant were shut tight - it appeared as if Lord Shiva Himself was deeply engrossed in the state of meditation!

In a further mysterious development, the lamp in the labour room went out soon after the birth of the Divine child. Surprisingly, the room still remained aglow with a soothing illumination - and at the same time, there began a mysterious shower of fragrant Lotus seeds all around Kashishwari Devi and her new-born son!

Soon, the whole room got filled with the sweet aroma of the Lotus flowers and to add to the wonder, the characteristic sound of wooden sandals softly moving atop the roof, could also be heard distinctly! All these magical signs gave clear proof of the special nature of the new-born infant! It also became clear that the monk Vilayat Ali had arrived in subtle form, to bless this Divine child!

And shortly thereafter, the new-born infant broke its worrisome silence and began to cry vigorously - on hearing that welcome sound, everyone in the household was overjoyed with relief!

It is well-known that miraculous incidents had preceded the Divine birth of each and every Incarnation of God Supreme. For example, all of us are familiar with the entire chain of charming events that took place, just after the Divine birth of Bhagavan Sri Krishna in the prison of King Kamsa in Mathura. Similar magical events had preceded the birth of Bhagavan Buddha Dev also. And now, the same was true for the Divine birth of Bhagavan Satyananda Dev too!

On getting to know about such Divine happenings, we always get filled with a lingering sense of awe - for us, such events are direct evidence of the Grace of God in human life!

And now we shall turn our attention to the growing-up years of Sri Thakur...the Leela that happened during this period is equally wonderful as well!

“Go on performing your duty while constantly praying to God and repeating His Holy Name.” - Sri Thakur

CHAPTER THREE

The Leela of Growing-up Period

Friends, let us start getting to know more about the wonderful Leela that happened during the growing-up period of Sri Thakur. For the sake of convenience, we shall describe it in three phases:

1. Early Childhood:

With time, the Divinely blessed infant grew up into a child of lovable appearance. He was duly given the name of 'Satyabrata', which means the one, who always abides by truth - this was indeed the most appropriate description of an 'Avatar'.

And the loveliness of this child was comparable to that of a beautiful bloom of rose - everyone fell in love with him at the first sight! As a result, he soon became the apple of the eyes of not only everyone in his own family but that of his neighbours as well.

By the time he turned three years old, Satyabrata had grown up into a child given to much mischief. So, he always had to be kept under constant watch. But given his naughty nature, Satyabrata's childhood soon came to be marked by many distinguishing incidents. One of them is related below:

One day, the mischievous child managed to give a slip to the alert eyes of his caretaker while playing outside. In a naughty mood, Satyabrata made a big jump from the elevated porch of his house onto the road below. But his playful antics that day resulted in an injury as his head got accidentally hit against a roadside manhole. However, despite being hurt, he remained unperturbed without uttering even a single cry - this was truly unusual for a small child of his tender age!

Later on, Kashishwari Devi got the shock of her life when she suddenly discovered congealed blood on the scalp of her dear son while feeding him on her lap. On subsequent interrogation of the caretaker, the worried mother came to know about the above incident - the wound of the child was at once washed, medicated and dressed up.

But in a sign of fascinating fortitude for such a small child, not even one drop of tear was shed by him, even while his wound was getting treated with astringent medicines! In the future too, such remarkable feats of endurance would continue to be displayed by Satyabrata, all through his growing up period. All these Divine portents gave a very clear indication: he was a born Yogi!

The Divine essence of Satyabrata became evident in another arena: playfulness. While other children of similar age usually love to play ordinary games, Satyabrata's play was of a different nature altogether. One of his favourite games was to do the role-play of 'Dhyana'. In this unusual game, Satyabrata used to take up the role of a monk lost in meditation while his younger brother used to play the role of his disciple. And during such times, his noble appearance as he sat with eyes closed used to closely resemble the

Divinity of Lord Shiva himself!

Often, as the Divine child used to start meditating, he used to get completely motionless. And in that absorbed state, he used to perceive his subtle inner essence escaping towards the infinitude of the sky, from within the shackles of his gross physical body. In fact, from high up in the sky, he could see his own body sitting immobile in a state of 'Dhyana'.

And after the lapse of a finite duration of time, his subtle inner essence used to come back into his body. The unusual nature of such a meditative experience used to make him quite nervous - he used to worry if he was suffering from some mental aberration!

Much later, the Divine child - Satyabrata grew up into the foremost Saint of our times, Sri Thakur Satyananda and in the initial period of his 'Sadhana', he used to remain engrossed in the state of 'Dhyana' for 18 to 20 hours each day! And in that state, Sri Thakur used to get blessed with 'Samadhi'. Only then, he could finally understand that he used to experience the same state of 'Samadhi' in his childhood also.

2. Middle Childhood:

Satyabrata's character used to shine with numerous virtues right from childhood - indomitable courage was the foremost among them. A wonderful example can be cited here.

Once he was walking along the borders of a rice field, deeply absorbed in his thoughts. All of a sudden, he was confronted with the frightening spectacle of a deadly cobra with its big hood up in the air, blocking his path. Any other child would have been terrified by the very sight of such menace. However, Satyabrata was fearless by nature - he just stood for a moment to consider his action in the face of that fearsome danger.

And thereafter, he performed an extraordinarily brave act: keeping his nerves steady, he simply jumped over the hooded snake and landed on the other side of the cobra! Then, he just sprinted away to safety. His bravery was witnessed and appreciated by all the farmers working nearby - they were simply astounded by the courage of a small child in the face of such peril!

Another novel quality of Satyabrata was his deep fascination with science and all its marvels. This Divine child had a passion for imagining scientific inventions, completely unheard of, in his time. For example, this gifted child had already solved the complexities of building submarine, torpedo, helicopter and so many other technological wonders! It was a sheer miracle that he could unravel the mysteries of such big inventions so early in his life!

And he was not content with just contemplating those scientific inventions - he took great care to test their practicality as well! Towards this end, for example, this gifted child used to first build working models of a submarine and then, investigate their efficacy in the waters of the bathing tank of his own house!

All the incidents described above are just the tip of the iceberg of his childhood Leela...reams of pages will be required just to touch upon them!

3. Schooling Years: -

Moral uprightness, love and compassion were the trademark virtues of Satyabrata. Under their noble influence, he used to make friends with boys of good character in his school (the renowned Hindu school of Calcutta) and constantly emphasize to them the value of cultivating morality in all spheres of life.

His innate love and compassion became visible quite early during this period, as shown by the following chain of events:

Once Satyabrata came to know that one of his friends was sick. Immediately, he decided to go to that friend's house to enquire about his well-being. So, one day, setting aside his morning routine of going to school, he went to his friend's house instead. A few boys from his friend circle accompanied him as well.

After reaching the house, Satyabrata conveyed his deep empathy and care by softly caressing the thin body of his friend. Neither any word could be exchanged due to the doctor's order nor was any word necessary as all communication took place from heart to heart. Thereafter, the boys sorrowfully came out and quietly proceeded toward their school.

On reaching their destination, they found that their classes had already started. And as Satyabrata reached his class, he got rebuked by his teacher for his tardiness and was made to sit on the last bench of the classroom as punishment. Then the class resumed, but Satyabrata could not concentrate on what was being taught, as he was continuously thinking about his sick friend. The whole of his mind was overflowing with compassion for his friend.

All of a sudden, Satyabrata was put to a stern test, when his teacher could make out that he was not paying attention in the class - the annoyed teacher began to quiz him on what had been taught in the class since the very beginning. And to the amazement of his teacher and classmates alike, he could correctly answer every question!

The pleased teacher soon came to know about the benevolent reason behind Satyabrata's unusual delay in reaching school that day. At once, the remorseful teacher reversed his earlier punishment and allowed Satyabrata to come forward and resume his usual seat at the very front of the class. In this manner, the whole incident ended on a happy note and as they say, all is well that ends well!

It is aptly said that morning shows the day: the innate virtues of God- Incarnates always become apparent right from their childhood. This is true for each 'Avatar': Bhagavan Sri Ramachandra, Bhagavan Sri Krishna, Bhagavan Sri Buddha... And, as we saw, this is true for Bhagavan Satyananda Dev as well!

"The way is faith: faith in the Grace of God." - Sri Thakur

CHAPTER FOUR

Earnest Spiritual Endeavours

All Incarnates carry the seed of Godliness within them since their birth - at the appropriate time, this seed sprouts and starts giving rise to a gigantic tree of Spirituality, that would give shade and comfort to the entire humanity one day. And as we'll see in this Chapter, this eternal principle was very much true for Sri Thakur also.

Satyabrata, in due course of time, finished his schooling and got enrolled in college to pursue higher education. Right from this point of time onward, he made up his mind to opt for the sacred path of 'Sanyas' and eschew the trifling pleasures of worldly life. The inner urge for this path, ever-present since his childhood, got transformed into a firm resolve at the starting point of his college.

So, on one hand, he regularly attended college; on the other hand, he continued his 'Sadhana' at the same pace at home. And now the sacred books of scriptures began to accompany him always: studying them frequently became his habit.

The noble path of spirituality thus came to co-exist with academics in his daily routine - during the day, he used to studiously attend his classes at college and on coming back home, he used to go back to his ‘Sadhana’. Now, I shall relate a thrilling incident to illustrate the astounding level of his concentration during this ‘Sadhana’!

One day, he was sitting in his room, completely absorbed in ‘Dhyana’. And after a while, his younger sister happened to come in with a bowl of milk for him. However, she got the fright of her life to discover that a huge cobra was already present in that room and the deadly serpent had spread its massive hood over her brother’s head! The bowl slipped from her shaking hand and her desperate cries for help alerted the rest of the household, who rushed to Satyabrata’s room! Fortunately, this terrifying spectacle came to end after a while, as the cobra lowered its hood on its own and disappeared quietly.

The whole scenario represented nothing short of Divine symbolism: it indicated to everyone that Satyabrata was Lord Shiva Himself - that’s why the cobra, His ever-faithful companion had appeared to pay its respect to the Lord Supreme! And, many such unusual events continued to occur, all of which pointed out to Satyabrata’s Divine nature. In this manner, his Godly nature started gradually unfolding before his entire family!

In due course of time, Satyabrata completed his Intermediate, Bachelor’s and Master’s degree from the University of Calcutta. During this period, as his ‘Sadhana’ kept on increasing in intensity, it did not escape the attention of his alarmed family, who got worried that he would become a monk in the future and leave them forever. Therefore, his well-off family started trying their best to bring him back to the lures of the material world, through the temptation of marriage. Satyabrata, however, firmly refused despite facing repeated scolding from his father.

And at times, such family pressure used to get so intense, that once he even tried to end his life by trying to jump off the terrace of his house. Luckily, in the nick of time, his youngest brother managed to grab hold of him from the back and thus, save his life. Ultimately, Satyabrata's steadfast resolve to remain celibate, made his family capitulate. And thereafter, no further pressure was brought upon him for entering into marital bondage.

In this context, we recall how Bhagavan Buddha Dev grew up amidst the abundance of a kingdom and yet chose to renounce all such material riches in favour of the noble path of 'Sanyas'. The same trend was now visible in the life of Bhagavan Satyananda Dev also.

In this manner, every stage in the life of a God-Incarnate serves as a role model. That is why the study of such a sacred life is so valuable for us.

"The main thing is to surrender to God. He always protects the one who surrenders to him." - Sri Thakur

CHAPTER FIVE

Magnificent Awakening of Divinity Within

Friends, from this chapter onwards, we enter into the Divine realm of the spiritual transformation of Satyabrata into Sri Thakur Satyananda. So, come, let us know more about this sacred metamorphosis process...

As Satyabrata's family gave up its efforts to get him married, he continued his 'Sadhana' with full fervour. Its intensity was truly remarkable! For example, in the heat of peak summer, he used to sit (without any cushion mat) on the searingly hot surface of the open terrace of his house at midday and in addition, wrap a warm quilt over his body for creating additional hotness! Then, in that blazing heat, he used to go on performing 'Japa' for hours together!

In a like manner, he used to sit for a long duration in the biting chill of winter on the bitterly cold surface of the same terrace and wrap up himself in a wet cloth to escalate the freezing cold! And then, he used to go on performing 'Japa' for a long duration!

Many a time, he used to repeatedly hit himself hard on the back with a wooden dumbbell for increasing his power of tolerance to pain! And, he used to go on practically starving himself day after day, by having just a small amount of boiled pulses in the morning and a little milk in the evening. And not even a drop of water used to pass his lips during the college hours!

Initially, as part of his 'Sadhana', Satyabrata used to meditate on formless 'Nirakar Brahma'. It was just like the 'Sadhana' of a 'Yogi' in 'Sanatan Dharma'. But one day, it so happened that while he was immersed in such 'Sadhana', a calendar picture of Divine Mother, 'Maa' came flying through the air and landed precisely on his lap. It happened all of a sudden. Now, this was a strange happening, to say the least, as no breeze of any kind was blowing inside the room, then!

As a startled Satyabrata quickly picked up the picture, he came to understand in a flash that, from then onwards he was being spiritually directed, to pursue the path of 'Sadhana' on the Divine Form of 'Maa'. Thereafter, Satyabrata decided to change the direction of his 'Sadhana'. He got that picture of 'Maa' framed and respectfully installed on the throne of sanctum sanctorum of his worship room. And then, he proceeded in the new direction of his spiritual practise with zeal. In due course, his 'Sadhana' got blessed through the Holy Vision of 'Maa'.

To further accelerate his 'Sadhana', Satyabrata decided to seek spiritual initiation from His Holiness Swami Abhedananda, one of the last surviving disciples of Bhagavan Ramakrishna Dev. So, one day he set out for 'Vedanta Math', the holy Ashram of Swami Abhedananda ji in Kolkata and on reaching there, he offered homage to his future Guru, who was taken by surprise to note the sharp contrast between his shabby outer appearance and his distinguished family background!

Afterwards, as both talked together, Abhedananda ji could gauge the sincerity of Satyabrata's spiritual yearning.

And subsequently, on an auspicious day, he blessed Satyabrata with sacred 'Mantra Diksha'. Satyabrata's elder brother also had the good luck of being initiated by his holiness Abhedananda ji.

The spiritual zeal of Satyabrata kept increasing day by day. Sacred feelings of purity and renunciation constantly arose within his mind. In due course, everyone in his family began to revere him just like the holy image of God Himself. They were spellbound by the wonderful glow of spirituality that completely animated his entire being. Each of them came to gradually realize that Satyabrata had transcended the limited confines of his immediate family. Now he had become the source of Divine sustenance for the whole world. It was a truly remarkable happening!

After a while, Swami Abhedananda ji happened to establish his new Ashram (along with school and other facilities) in the scenic town of Darjeeling in north Bengal. He decided that Satyabrata would be the right choice as the head of this newly opened Ashram. But when he conveyed his decision to Satyabrata, he came to know that latter's family might not agree to release him.

Hence, Abhedananda ji came to Satyabrata's house to ask if his 'Shishya' would be released for the proposed assignment. Immediately his grandmother, father, mother etc. began to cry in unison and urged Swami Abhedananda ji not to take away Satyabrata, the apple of their eyes. However, they promised that he would be given unfettered liberty at home to pursue his chosen path of 'Tapasya'.

His Holiness Abhedananda ji, moved by such tremendous respect displayed by everyone in the family towards Satyabrata, blessed his 'Shishya' and directed him as follows, "Satyabrata, you will succeed in your 'Sadhana' in your home itself - you need not go anywhere else".

Satyabrata, who deeply admired his Guru ji, followed this instruction faithfully all through his life.

Thereafter, Satyabrata continued on his chosen path of 'Sadhana' with full dedication, while continuing to stay back at home, as advised by his Guru ji. And slowly, he came to look upon his family members as his devotees! However, he removed all physical contact with them to the extent feasible and kept himself aloof within his separate room in the house.

Here he used to remain completely absorbed in 'dhyana' day-in and day-out and nobody could come except on absolute necessity. In addition, 'Puja room' on the second floor of the house was also kept specially reserved for him. In this manner, he kept preparing himself for 'Sanyas', the all-renouncing life of Monkhood.

Days passed and then came the most important day in the life of Satyabrata. For this occasion, he got a piece of garment, dyed in ochre colour - the sacred colour of 'Sanyas'. Wearing the garment, he went upstairs to the Puja room, shut its door and began his 'Sadhana' in the right earnest - throughout that night he kept performing the holy ritual of 'Homa', along with continuous prayers to Maa to bless his spiritual endeavours.

At an auspicious moment in the early hours of the morning, his prayer was granted: Maa Herself appeared before him and blessed him with the boon of 'Sanyas'. And She also blessed him with a new monastic name, 'Satyananda' - he thus gradually came to be known as Sri Thakur Satyananda among all his devotees, disciples and followers.

In earlier incarnations, Bhagavan Buddha Dev and Bhagavan Chaitanya Dev both had chosen to first renounce their family and then adopt the path of 'Sanyas'. A new trail was now created by Bhagavan Satyananda Dev, who chose to stay back with his family in his own home and then, continue his 'Sadhana', which ultimately led to his getting blessed with 'Sanyas' by his Divine Mother.

And just as the first glimmer of dawn on the horizon results in a dazzling day afterwards, likewise the small spring of Spirituality (that first came into public view with the opening of Sri Thakur's first Ashram at the town of Suri in 1939) gave rise to a vast ocean of Spiritual bliss in due course of time.

In the next few chapters, we shall be tasting a few drops of this ocean of Divine 'Amrit'.

"Just go on repeating Holy Name of God - just go on praying to Him - He will make everything alright." - Sri Thakur

Part 2

Sri Thakur's Divine Glory - A Glimpse

CHAPTER SIX

Upholding 'Dharma', the Spinal Cord of India

Friends, Sri Thakur's Spiritual aura is so immense and multi-faceted that, we can only stand in awe in front of this vast ocean. So come, let us taste just a few drops of this nectar of Divinity and make our lives blessed...

1. Ashram

The lotus of the Spiritual genius of Sri Thakur began to bloom in a beautiful manner, as he continued his 'Sadhana' at his ancestral house at Suri, a town of Birbhum district in undivided Bengal. Slowly his silent 'Tapasya' began to attract the attention of spiritual seekers and they began coming in increasing numbers to seek his holy company. In due course of time, Sri Thakur established his first Ashram in that very house in 1939.

The unique feature of this Ashram was the fact that, besides adult devotees, many children used to come here every day, pulled-in by the Divine attraction of Sri Thakur.

They used to love taking part in daily fun and games with Sri Thakur and the holy Ashram grounds used to, therefore, resound with the delightful sounds of laughter, clapping and merriment! And such fun and games became a channel of the flow of Spirituality from Sri Thakur to the tiny tots!

The daily activities of Ashram used to revolve around Puja, Japa, Dhyana, Arati, 'Mantra Diksha', Kirtan, Spiritual discourses, Cultural programs...it was a holistic picture of Spiritual life. The exemplary life of Sri Thakur himself was the biggest inspiration for everyone. Intense 'Tapasya' was the hallmark of his Divine life: a lion's share (18 to 20 hours!) of 24 hours in a day used to be earmarked by him for God while bodily necessities such as eating, sleeping etc. were relegated to the bare minimum! In a nutshell, his life on a day-to-day basis was truly Divine!

Over a period of time, Sri Thakur's spiritual fragrance spread with establishment of branch Ashrams at many places in Bengal such as Batikaar, Dubrajpur, Baranagar, Rampurhat, Kandi etc. and that in Bihar such as Madhupur, Dumka etc. All these Ashrams soon became the fulcrum of spiritual nourishment for large section of people.

"Strict discipline, integrity and hard work are what are needed." - Sri Thakur

2. Puja

Ashram life revolves around worship of God through 'Puja' - it is performed both on daily basis as well as on special occasions of the calendar. And in Bengal, the biggest of such occasions happens to be the sacred Durga Puja, where Maa Durga is worshipped by her children over a period of five days in the autumn season.

Sri Mahendra Nath had earnestly wished that the holy ceremony of Durga Puja should be organized at Suri Ashram. On getting to know about his father's desire, Sri Thakur had prayed to Maa and received Her formal permission to organize 'Durga Puja' at Ashram. Four phases are visible in this celebration: -

First Phase: -

After receiving permission of Maa, the first Durga Puja was organized in September 1941. A beautiful ten-armed traditional image of Maa Durga was brought over from Kolkata and worshipped at the holy Ashram premises with the highest devotion. On such occasions, it was Maa Sarada, who was symbolically worshipped in the image of Maa Durga. The holy offering of flowers at the feet of Maa Durga used to be offered with a special mantra addressed to Maa Sarada. The annual ritual continued in this form till 1949.

Second Phase: -

From 1950 onwards, the next phase started with the completely new tradition of performing all the rituals of Puja in front of an actual image of Maa Sarada Herself. Initially, many devotees felt disheartened on the discontinuation of the traditional form of Sri Durga Puja. Then under Sri Thakur's Grace, they finally came to understand that Maa Durga was, in real essence, a manifestation of Maa Sarada herself. His inspiring words cheered up everyone and in due course, the Ashram grounds overflowed with large crowds, eager to witness such a unique form of Sri Durga Puja.

Third Phase: -

The image worshipped so far during Sri Durga Puja underwent a change in 1955. It had an interesting history behind it. The auspicious birth centenary of Maa Sarada came around in the year of 1954. To mark this memorable occasion, Sri Thakur began the tradition of organizing a large fair named 'Sarada Mela' in the town of Suri. An elegant image of Maa Sarada was specially crafted and then, installed in the main pavilion of that fair.

And from 1955 onwards, it was this image of Maa Sarada, which was worshipped during Sri Durga Puja at Ashram. Since this image was so graceful in appearance, Sri Thakur decided to keep it back at Ashram and not allow it to be immersed in water, as customarily done at the end of the celebration.

Fourth and the final phase: -

This phase commenced in 1958 when Sri Thakur received instructions from Maa that Sri Durga Puja should be started at Baranagar Ashram also. The idol of Maa Sarada was accordingly shifted from Suri to Baranagar. And in a unique practice, eight more hands were then added to this two-armed image, making it a ten-armed Image, holding one weapon in each hand. This wonderful ten-armed 'Sarada-Durga' Idol was then ceremonially worshipped over the customary five-day period.

Thus began the sacred tradition of Sri Sarada-Durga Puja at Baranagar Ashram, which continues till date, with the same purity of devotion, even after the passage of so many decades.

In like manner, the sacred Image of Maa Sarada is worshipped throughout the year as Sri Lakshmi, Sri Kali and so on. It is a really befitting way of respecting Maa Sarada in different manifestations of her own Divine self and stands as a unique contribution of Sri Thakur in the annals of Religion and Spirituality.

"Just go on repeating Holy Name of God at all times." - Sri Thakur

3. The Beautiful Leela of Sri Gopal ji

In the Divine life of Sri Thakur, one of the loveliest chapters is the delightful Leela of Sri Gopal Ji. This was a tiny idol that had arrived in the household of Sri Mahendra Nath just a few days before the birth of Sri Thakur. Later on, that holy icon of Sri Gopal ji was brought over from the Kashipur household and ceremonially installed at Baranagar Ashram.

Thereafter, so many unbelievable instances of Divine Leela of Sri Gopal ji took place. Some of the instances are joyfully shared here.

Now, Gopal ji was very fond of watching the cultural programs, that were so tastefully arranged at Baranagar Ashram, round the year on different occasions. In this sequence, an all-night music program was being held at Baranagar once and Sri Gopal ji was happily listening to the songs of the artist on the dais, while cosily held in the lap of one of the Sanyasini mothers.

After a while, Gopal ji was lovingly put to sleep by his Sanyasini mother as he was literally looked upon as a living entity at the holy Ashram. And it is a well-known custom in India that, a small infant like Gopal ji is not supposed to remain awake the whole night. He is supposed to undergo refreshing sleep. But lo and behold! To the amazement of everyone, it was discovered that Gopal ji had sat up on his own, soon after he was put in his sleeping bed! Immediately, Sri Thakur gave the instruction that Gopal ji should be taken to the venue of the music program once again: He would like to enjoy the rest of the program as well!

In the same astonishing manner, Gopal ji would inevitably sit up during each and every journey by train or by car, while accompanying Sri Thakur. It used to straight away imply that, just like any other small kid, he also wanted to relish the passing sceneries of Mother Nature. So, his Sanyasini mother would oblige and hold Gopal ji in her lap, as He happily soaked in the natural sceneries from the train or car window!

Now, Gopal ji was always treated to homemade sweets as a compulsory part of his daily worship. But once it so happened that, the bowl of milk meant for preparing his sweets, somehow slipped down from the hands of his Sanyasini mother. So, no milk was available anymore for preparing the sweets for Gopal ji. Nor could any milk be purchased, as all the shops were closed in that afternoon hour.

And the Sanyasini mothers did not want to disturb Sri Thakur. This was because, as per the past precedent, he would inevitably instruct that a little milk, kept reserved for his own consumption, should be used to prepare sweets for his beloved Gopal ji instead! So, this option was ruled out as well.

Hence, the Sanyasini mothers began earnestly praying to Gopal ji for a solution that satisfies everybody. Suddenly it was discovered, to the utter joy of the worried Sanyasini mothers that, a cow and calf had arrived on their own - they were found to be patiently standing in the heat of afternoon sun near the closed main gate of the Ashram!

That milch cow was recognized to be the same one that was brought in by the milkman to Ashram daily evening. Sanyasini mothers, overjoyed at this completely unexpected blessing, quickly arranged for the gate to be opened - the two animals then rushed in and the milch cow came to stand at that very spot where she used to wait during her daily milking hour. It was just astonishing!

Then the milkman, who was happily asleep at that hour in his home, was sent for. The amazed milkman came in reluctantly, thinking all the while, what was his milch cow doing at Ashram at that odd hour and wondering if she would give any milk in that afternoon heat! Again, a miracle happened: on that day, she yielded milk, that was far in excess of what she used to normally give on other days! And that quantity was more than sufficient for the preparation of sweets for dear Gopal ji! Divine magic was happening in front of the eyes of everyone!

Sri Thakur was delighted when this wonderful chain of events was related to him by equally happy Sanyasini mothers! He joyfully exclaimed, 'Look, it is our beloved Gopal ji Himself, who listened to your heartfelt prayers. It is his Divine Mercy that has made all these miracles possible!'

In such a manner, Gopal ji kept showering His Divine Grace. It is a truly glorious tale of Divine bliss!

"Puja needs to be performed - God has mandated it." - Sri Thakur

4. Daily Spiritual Discourse

Sri Thakur was like a giant spiritual magnet, whose unseen yet powerful aura used to attract so many devotees every day. This used to hold good for whichever Ashram Sri Thakur used to be stationed at any point of time: Baranagar, Suri or other Ashrams.

And then an event of tremendous goodness used to occur there multiple times a day: Sri Thakur, the God Incarnate Himself, used to read and explain the sacred words of God, contained in our holy Scriptures! Those sacred words, uttered by God Himself earlier and explained by God-Incarnate Himself (i.e., Sri Thakur) then, used to directly reach the ears of the fortunate devotees present...! Truly, how glorious this phenomenon was!

These Scriptures compulsorily included the holy trio of Srimad Bhagwat Gita, Sri Ramakrishna Kathamrita, and Upanishad. And as per the occasion, other holy books such as Sri Chaitanya Charitamrita, Sri Ramakrishna Mangal Kavya etc. were also read. And Sri Thakur had a unique method of conducting such discourses:

First, a portion of the concerned Scripture used to be read out and then, Sri Thakur used to explain that text in the light of Spirituality as well as science. Sri Thakur thus introduced the novel idea of explaining our ancient scriptures in terms of modern science! So, his discourses marked the wonderful blending of ancient Scriptural wisdom and modern Scientific knowledge!

And in a new twist, Sri Thakur used to often ask, at random, any devotee present as to what he had learnt that day. This custom had the salutary effect of keeping everyone alert during the entire duration of the discourse, as they knew beforehand that Sri Thakur could ask them questions at any moment.

Plus, as Sri Thakur used to emphasize so often, God is present within the heart of each one of us. So, a fresh perspective on the topic at hand used to emerge each and every time, a devotee used to answer the question posed by Sri Thakur!

As a result, the total atmosphere of those blissful discussions used to get enriched immeasurably! How wonderful the whole session used to be!

“Every day, all of you should take pains and ensure that ‘Japa’ should go on within your mind at all times amidst whatever you do.” - Sri Thakur

5. *Sadhu Sammelan*

Sri Thakur was a firm believer in the concept of unity in the diversity of Hinduism. He gave this concept a unique name: United Nations organization, U.N.O of Religion. Basically, he wished that the followers of each particular path of Hinduism should adhere to their respective path and at the same time, respect other paths as well. That would bring in the much-needed unity within Hinduism, the faith of the majority in India.

Towards the fulfilment of this noble mission, Sri Thakur used to periodically invite the respected Sanyasis and Sanyasini Mothers, representing different Ashrams of Hinduism. These respected religious figures used to gather together in a unique "Sadhu Sammelan" on the holy grounds of Sri Thakur's Ashram and then discuss some selected topics of Hinduism in the sacred presence of Sri Thakur himself. In this sequence, so many renowned Spiritual heads of different monasteries such as Sanyasini Durga Puri Maa, Sanyasini Gayatri Maa, Sri Mohanananda Brahmachari and others had come over on different occasions.

Sri Thakur used to repeatedly stress that it was the bounden duty of each individual, following any particular sect of Hinduism, to enhance the effectiveness of the U.N.O of Hinduism. He was very clear in his mind that the cultivation of Spirituality in life by an individual is not meant for the uplifting of only his own self. Rather Spirituality is meant for the welfare of everyone. That is why he had given the clarion call for the formation of the U.N.O of Hinduism.

And, in his invaluable opinion, the wonderful concept of 'global togetherness', as given in our holy Upanishad was the most appropriate philosophy for such U.N.O of Hinduism to come into practical existence.

"Through the habit of constant remembrance of God, we can create new channels of devotion to God in our brain. That is why Bhagavan Sri Krishna has laid so much stress upon 'Abhyas Yoga' in Gita."- Sri Thakur

6. Mani Mandir

A long-cherished dream of Sri Thakur was realised with the inauguration of the temple of 'Mani Mandir' at Baranagar Ashram on 13th March 1967. Now, 'Mani Mandir' means the jewel temple - indeed this glass-walled temple used to shine like a sparkling jewel at night! And this beauty used to get enhanced even more by the reflection of that shining effulgence on the flowing waters of the holy river Ganga, on the bank of which Baranagar Ashram is located!

The principal Deity of this new temple was Maa Trinayani (a new form of Maa Kali), whose looks had flashed before Sri Thakur in the form of a 'Divine Vision'. And this appearance was quite different from the conventional appearance of Maa Kali. The holy name 'Trinayani' was given by Sri Thakur too.

Maa Trinayani is a four-armed Deity, blue in complexion, who holds a sword of lightning in one hand, while 'Kamandalu' (a pitcher of holy water) is there in Her second hand. Her other two hands shower blessings on devotees. And she stands on a beautiful lotus flower (instead of Lord Shiva) - altogether She has an unusual yet beautifully Divine appeal.

Sri Thakur used to look upon Maa Trinayani just like his own daughter and was very fond of decorating Her with costly ornaments and new dresses every day. Very interestingly, She used to tell Sri Thakur when Her decoration on any particular day was not up to Her liking. Then, as per Sri Thakur's instruction, new ornamentation had to be arranged for Her immediately. And, because She was considered to be a maiden by Sri Thakur, the red vermillion mark (an external symbol of married state) was never used for her adornment.

Then there also used to be joyful days, when Trinayani Maa used to be very happy with Her particular attire. Her delight used to get transmitted to Sri Thakur who then used to exclaim in bliss, "Just see! How radiantly beautiful does Maa look! She is truly glad today!" In this manner, a wonderful Leela used to go on between the God Incarnate Sri Thakur Satyananda and his beloved daughter, Trinayani Maa.

"We are all children of bliss - we have come to this Earth to stay on the path of bliss - at the end, we shall all go back to that eternal source of bliss." - Sri Thakur

7. Holy Name of God

The whole cosmos is vibration in its true essence and God is the Highest vibration, whose manifestation occurs in the form of the Word. That is why Word is God and God is Word. Hence, God and His sacred Name are one and the same. So, when we sincerely utter the Holy Name of God, then we are blessed by the Divine touch of God himself.

This is why all Incarnations of God in every single age have extolled the virtue of uttering the Holy Name of God at all times. In this modern age, Sri Thakur had also upheld the sanctity of the constant utterance of the Holy Name of God. He had always advised his devotees to take recourse to this all-powerful means for making steady progress on the Spiritual path.

"For getting complete fortification, it is important to pray to God, read sacred scriptures, cultivate noble thoughts, and always carry the Holy Image of God with oneself."- Sri Thakur

8. Tapasya

Spiritual austerity, 'Tapasya' was the hallmark of the sacred life of Sri Thakur and all his renunciate disciples (Sannyasi and Sanyasini Mothers) as well. The special features of this multi-faceted 'Tapasya' are highlighted here:

- Sri Thakur used to repeatedly emphasize that 'Tapasya', voluntary self-denial was the only means through which the dormant seed of Spirituality could be awakened within us and the gross desires of our physical body curbed.
- This is why Sri Thakur used to consider 'Tapasya' as desirable for all spiritual seekers in general and mandatory for spiritual renunciates in particular.
- On the day of Ekadashi (the 11th day of the lunar fortnight), Sri Thakur used to keep fast and observe complete silence for the whole day. The same example used to be followed by all his disciples as well - they used to spend the day in Japa and Dhyana in total silence.
- Inspired by Sri Thakur, his disciples would regularly carry out Japa and Dhyana in the open courtyard of Ashrams in the peak of summer heat in the afternoon and in the height of winter chill at night.

- Similarly, those disciples used to often carry out 'Homa' during the entire night.
- Sometimes they used to sing 'Kirtan' throughout the night and even several nights together.
- And at other times, they used to stand on one foot and spend the whole night in carrying out Japa and Dhyana.
- These disciples also used to perform a novel form of Tapasya whereby they would go to a particular Temple, not by walking, but by nonstop rolling on the ground! This was called 'Dandi Tapasya' - in this process, their bodies used to get badly scratched but they would remain completely indifferent to such bodily pain and would silently go on repeating the Holy Name of God till they reached their destination!

And Sri Thakur's blessing would always get showered on all his disciples, who would willingly subject themselves to these harsh spiritual austerities, through the sacred path of 'Tapasya'.

"In the Spiritual matter, the very first thought that comes to mind needs to be listened to and in the worldly affair, it is the second thought striking the mind that needs to be attended to."- Sri Thakur

CHAPTER SEVEN

Sowing the Seeds of Man-making Education

Swami Vivekananda famously said, "Education is the manifestation of perfection already in man". And Sri Thakur too was a firm believer in the astonishing power of such man-making education. That is why he had opened an informal school for little children at Suri Ashram since its inception. Some unique features of this school were:

- First, this institution came into existence with only ten children on its roll.
- Second, the little children used to attend their classes out in the open, on a mattress spread on the ground, near a fruit tree in the Ashram compound. There was no furniture in the conventional sense of a school!
- Third, the classes used to begin in a novel manner with 'dhyana'. The little children used to meditate with eyes closed, while Sri Thakur used to stroll about in the class with a lighted stick of aromatic incense in his hand. And these obedient children used to open their eyes, only on hearing the signal of 'Sri Hari Ramakrishna', chanted by Sri Thakur. This was unique indeed!

- The character of little children used to get enriched through daily moral instruction from Sri Thakur - he used to guide them in moulding their lives through the high ideals of constant devotion to God, their parents as well as their teachers.
- He also used to encourage these budding talents to have a high aim in life and start moving towards that aim right from their childhood.
- The powerful positive affirmation, "We shall grow up to be great" used to be daily chanted by him, for subsequent repetition by the little children. It was a very powerful auto-suggestion that used to profoundly impact their malleable minds.

Sri Thakur was a strong votary of education in the language of Sanskrit. He wanted to make the learning of Sanskrit compulsory at all levels as this Divine language contains the key to the formation of noble character through regular study of our holy scriptures written in Sanskrit.

So, in totality, 'Education' was held up by Sri Thakur as the best means of flowering of inborn talent of children and developing their character. For him, education was never meant to be degraded to a merely mechanical means of earning a living.

Keeping all these ideals in view, the school of 'Sri Ramakrishna Vidyapeeth' was established by Sri Thakur at Suri in 1942. Gradually, schools came to be established at other branch Ashrams as well.

And to impart higher education, Sri Thakur laid the foundation of 'Sri Abhedananda Mahavidyalaya' in the town of Sainthia in the Birbhum district.

Special Note:

Sri Thakur used to lay great emphasis on developing the unique talent of a child, granted to him by God, through the medium of education. For example, if a child was found to be good at writing poems and stories, then Sri Thakur used to encourage him to excel in that direction. And if a child was found good to be in music, Sri Thakur used to encourage her to further refine that God-given ability. In this manner, if a child was good in any domain of creativity, Sri Thakur used to encourage him or her all the way.

In this context, one of his most inspiring quotes is this: "The inner potential present within each individual is bound to flower to its full beauty provided that:

i. such potential should be exclusively meant for the worship of God and
ii. such potential should get developed through virtuous means."

That's why Sri Thakur used to encourage his disciples to constantly pray: "Maa, please make us fulfil the specific Mission, to accomplish which, You chose to send us to this earth".

And finally, mention must be made of the strong emphasis laid by Sri Thakur on "self-initiative" for learning any creative discipline. He used to firmly emphasise it was the only way in which the originality of God-given talent could be preserved.

"Always remember God is keeping watch over you - He is guiding you - keep this ever in mind."- Sri Thakur

CHAPTER EIGHT

Uplifting the Poor and the Downtrodden

If we were ever to describe Sri Thakur in one word, then we can straightaway say he was the living personification of the virtue of "compassion".

As an instance of his innate generosity, during his college days, he used to give tuition free of cost to a large number of poor students and provide them with books and monetary assistance, as and when required.

Even animals used to be recipients of his love and compassion. For example, one day he came across a sick and hungry stray dog while going to his college. His boundless empathy made him immediately get down from his bicycle and purchase some eatables from a nearby shop. Thereafter, with deep affection, he fed the starving animal with his own hand. Only then did he resume the journey to his college.

Many other incidents can be cited as well. All of them clearly revealed the inherently loving nature of Sri Thakur.

And inspired by him, his Sannyasi disciples also used to joyfully plunge into the noble arena of 'service to humanity' encompassing multiple forms such as providing food to the hungry during famines, distributing medicines to the afflicted throughout pandemics such as cholera, giving clothing to the poor during festivals, supplying medicines to the needy from the charitable Ashram dispensary etc.

He used to always uphold the golden principle of 'serving God by serving humanity' (given by Bhagavan Sri Ramakrishna Dev) by exhorting his disciples: "Whenever you are providing a hungry person with food, then think that you are making food offering to God Himself. And similarly, when you are distributing clothing among the needy, do so with the complete belief that God himself is standing in front of you. You are serving Him directly by helping such destitute people."

Here we can also share the exemplary way in which Sri Thakur used to arouse the inherent dignity of the so-called "untouchables", so cruelly treated in our society for a long time. In every village of Bengal and Bihar, where Ashrams were set up by Sri Thakur, he used to take special care to bring such marginalized people back into the main fold of the society. And he always chose the Divine path of spirituality to carry out this noble mission.

Sri Thakur used to re-ignite the sense of self-respect among them by naming them 'Thakur Das' (servant of God) and assuring them that any occupation they pursue after uttering the Holy Name of God is a worthy one. In this context, we will be honoured to know that he had held a special ceremony in the Batikaar village of Birbhum district, wherein a large number of these so-called "low caste untouchables" had received the Grace of Sri Thakur, in front of the holy sacrificial fire.

And after this ceremony, a few of them such as Chaitanya Dhangar had started leading such an admirably pure life that they became eligible to receive the highest blessings of 'Sanyas Deeksha'!

Friends, it is truly uplifting to share with you these noble steps initiated by Sri Thakur in the cause of serving humanity at large.

"Infinite power lies within you - you can do everything - all obstacles are bound to prostrate themselves before you."
- Sri Thakur

CHAPTER NINE

Blending together Science and Spirituality

Sri Thakur was a genius in the true sense of the word. One of the strongest indicators to support this statement would be his outstanding scientific temperament which was a part of his innate nature. That's why, he was so fond of carrying out innovative experiments in science, right from his childhood. And later on, when he was firmly established in the path of Spirituality, then he used to love applying scientific concepts in this sacred arena also. How unique this was in the spiritual tradition of our country...!

For example, when devotees used to plead before Sri Thakur about their inability to achieve the requisite concentration during their daily 'Dhyana', he used to make them sit in front of multi-coloured bulbs and meditate. The colour of such bulb - white, light blue, green, yellow, red - used to be chosen by him as per the individual devotee's basic nature. In this manner, he experimented with different colours and got good results in getting the desired level of concentration.

He used to love applying the concepts of various scientific disciplines such as physics, chemistry, biology, mathematics, psychology etc. to explain the abstract concepts of spirituality during his daily discourse. And he used to do it in such a manner that devotees with even non-science backgrounds could easily grasp his teachings. A few apt examples will serve to illustrate this point beautifully, though such instances are too numerous to be covered in this short account.

Let's take just one example: Sri Thakur used the concepts of Biology to explain the 5th shloka, the 10th chapter of the holy Gita. To bring out the inner essence of this shloka, he took the help of the relevant chapter of Botany which says that the leaves of lotus plants, growing in water, contain pores covered by a cutaneous layer, on top of which there is another waxy layer. As a result, water can never wet those lotus leaves, even though they are always surrounded by water.

In the same manner, Sri Thakur said, this water can be considered to represent the gross material world filled with temptations, while the waxy layer can be thought of as representing the protective covering of constant Devotion to God. So, a devotee remains untouched by the corrupting sins of this world due to the protective covering of the Grace of God.

Friends, there are numerous such examples given in the admirable volume entitled, "Vigyan manaska Satyananda" ("Scientific-minded Satyananda"), penned by revered Swami Hirananda ji in Bengali.

Suffice it to say that Sri Thakur magnificently combined the Eastern flavour of Spirituality and the Western flavour of Science to arrive at the total picture of Religion.

"God is very merciful in this age - He will shower His grace upon you if you make even the slightest efforts." - Sri Thakur

CHAPTER TEN

Creating Divine Literature

Sri Thakur was a vast Galaxy of knowledge with a constant quest to learn all throughout his life. His genius of learning found its expression through multifarious channels: writing books, composing poems, framing song lyrics, penning magazine articles, scripting drama, music drama, dance drama...the list just goes on.

Equally exemplary was the way he used to constantly encourage his monastic disciples to take up the pen and bring out their God-given talents by composing books, poems, songs etc. on their own. Thus, a rich treasury of Divine literature got built up in a short period, under the patronage of Sri Thakur. Let's now have a bird's eye view of this magnificent treasury:

1. Monthly Ashram magazine "Bhabmukhey"

This is the signature publication of Sri Thakur's Ashram that comes out every month in Bengali till date. Its longevity is noteworthy indeed! And the unique name of this magazine, whose inaugural issue got published on the auspicious 'tithi' of 'Guru Purnima' on 17th July 1943, is derived from the Bengali word "Bhabmukhey", (meaning: staying in bliss) connoting the blessing uttered by Mother Goddess to Bhagavan Sri Ramakrishna Dev at the sacred temple of Dakshineshwar.

The initial issues of this monthly publication used to contain articles, stories, poems etc. on Religion, Spirituality, Philosophy and allied topics, penned by Sri Thakur, Sanyasi disciples, Sanyasini Mother disciples, as well as other writers also. Now, this tradition is being continued by His successors at Ashram.

2. Books

Under Sri Thakur's Divine inspiration, a number of books began to be written, right from the inception of Suri Ashram. Examples of some initial publications of Ashram are: "Manjir" and "Bhajan Been". These publications contain collections of songs penned by Sri Thakur himself.

Sri Thakur always took a keen interest in the subject of Philosophy: he used to love brushing up his knowledge on the latest of this fascinating subject and teaching it to his disciples at Ashram. Under his encouragement, his foremost disciple - Sanyasini Archana Maa - initially wrote a series of articles in the monthly Ashram magazine, covering the gist of the important theories of Philosophy. Later on, as per the instructions of Sri Thakur, all these articles in Bengali were compiled into one single volume and duly published under the beautiful name, 'Samanvayi Darshan' (Integrated Philosophy).

Afterwards, Sri Thakur himself wrote a comprehensive three-part book series entitled 'World Philosophy', containing salient points of major schools of thought in Eastern as well as Western Philosophy. Later on, continuing this learned trend, he also composed two more magnificent book series entitled 'World Ethics' and 'World Psychology'. All of them represent heights of erudition and are of the greatest help to the earnest seekers of knowledge.

Simultaneously, Sri Thakur continued to express his inner Divinity in form of poetry as well as prose. A writer - lyricist par excellence, he penned more than seven thousand songs, hundreds of poems, essays, articles and several books of great spiritual calibre. His books are especially notable for bringing out the topics of Divinity in a beautifully aesthetic language. Currently, his collected works are available in eight volumes.

Mention must also be made of the contributions by the monastic disciples of Sri Thakur to the collection of Divine literature of Ashram. Under his Divine guidance, Sanyasini Archana Maa wrote books like 'Sri Ramakrishna Mangal Kavya'- the poetical biography of Bhagavan Sri Ramakrishna Dev, 'Janani Saradeshwari' - biography of Holy Mother Sri Sarada Devi, 'Sri Ramakrishna Gita', and composed many thousands of songs and poems too.

Similarly, Sanyasini mother Sharana Maa wrote an account of the illustrious life of Swami Vivekananda. Another Sanyasini mother, Arati Maa composed a seven-volume book series, entitled 'Sharavana-Mangalam' (Listening to Divine Bliss), in a date-wise diary format, covering the daily life and teachings of Sri Thakur over three decades. And there were more publications of other Sannyasi and Sanyasini mothers as well.

All in all, the Divine literature of Sri Thakur and his disciples continue to remain beacons of inspiration and joy for everyone aspiring to follow the path of Spirituality.

"We need to be geared towards God in body, mind and speech." - Sri Thakur

CHAPTER ELEVEN

Disseminating Divine Culture

Sri Thakur was an embodiment of exquisitely refined taste in all aspects of his day-to-day living. This found its expression through his appreciation for our rich heritage of art and culture. That's why he always wanted to preserve and enrich it through Spirituality.

He had an exceptionally broad outlook on art and culture. To him, all its wide-ranging forms such as music, dance, theatre, painting, sculpture, embroidery and even cooking were independent avenues for getting connected to God. This was a truly unique facet of the Divine personality of Sri Thakur!

The following narrative tries to briefly touch upon his glorious contributions to the propagation of Divine art and culture all through his illustrious life:

1. Music

For Swami Vivekananda, music was the highest form of worship. In the same tradition, Sri Thakur considered music as one of the holy paths to reach God. He was a true devotee of music himself and that is why so many artists of all-India repute used to love coming to Ashram and offering the homage of music at his lotus feet.

To fulfil this noble objective, a large number of renowned music artists came to him. They included Pandit Ravi Shankar, Pandit V G Jog, Pandit Omkarnath Thakur, Ustad Faiyaz Khan, Ustad Bade Ghulam Ali Khan, and so many others. Quite a few of them offered their musical tribute to Sri Thakur on more than one occasion.

Such devotion-soaked music, emanating straight from the heart of the artist, used to lead Sri Thakur to a deep state of meditation. And afterwards, he used to bless them in a mood of joy saying, "The beautiful music, you have offered just now, has reached my ears during my meditation and I have tried to transmit its sacred vibrations to the Divine Presence of God. Know for sure such Grace of God will greatly enhance the sweetness of your music".

Foreign musicians had also come to the holy presence of Sri Thakur quite a few times as if pulled in by the magnetic aura of that Divine personality. One such notable figure was Pete Seeger, the acclaimed folk musician from USA. He had visited the Dubrajpur Ashram and delighted Sri Thakur and all others present on that day with American folk music. And at the end, he had conclusively established that folk music of all countries have a commonality in their tunes.

One of the biggest qualities of Sri Thakur, already referred to earlier, was he knew how to encourage an individual artist and enable his potential to flower to its full glory. For example, Sri Rathin Ghosh was inspired by Sri Thakur to continuously polish his inborn talent of singing 'Kirtan' and subsequently, Sri Ghosh went on to earn the title of 'Kirtan Kalanidhi'.

Another instance can be cited about the exemplary way in which Sri Thakur used to give a boost to the folk music tradition of rural Bengal, especially its 'Baul' music tradition. He compiled lyrics of many such songs in folk dialects and catalysed the formation of a musician's group to promote this unique genre of music.

Most importantly, the musical genius of Sanyasini Archana Maa, the spiritual daughter of Sri Thakur, gradually bloomed to its full brilliance under the Divine guidance of her Guru and we have already made a mention of the thousands and thousands of songs composed by her.

And before concluding, we must mention how the holy ritual of 'Arati' used to be carried out in a uniquely musical manner in the Ashram temples. During this sacred ritual, a bouquet of devotional songs (composed by Sri Thakur, Sri Archana Maa and others) used to be offered as a musical homage to God. In Ashram, 'Arati' used to be performed several times every day and the tribute of music was offered each time.

During 'Arati', some of the songs were sung in solo by Sri Thakur and Archana Maa, while the rest were sung in chorus by Sanyasini mothers. And the musical accompaniment on 'Tabla' used to be done by a Sanyasi disciple of Sri Thakur, while other musical instruments such as sitar, organ and harmonium were played by Sanyasini mothers.

Such songs of devotion to God used to surcharge the entire atmosphere of Ashram and that of its surroundings with subtle vibrations of wonderful Divinity. Everyone could distinctly experience this sacred phenomenon day after day.

In this beautiful manner, Sri Thakur Satyananda literally built up a musical treasure chest of immense richness. These devotional songs, steeped in the eternal fragrance of Divinity, will forever remain an invaluable medium to connect all earnest Spiritual seekers to God.

"The more you cultivate noble thoughts - the more you perform noble deeds - the more 'holy man' you will become - the more 'whole man' you will become." - Sri Thakur

2. Dramatics

Sri Thakur, true to his genius, had conceived of the brilliant idea of utilizing non-conventional means such as theatre to spread the message of Spirituality all around. That is why he composed and directed many plays based on the Scriptures, sacred lives of God-Incarnates, holy lives of Saints, and other sources of Divinity. And he also motivated his monastic disciples such as Sri Archana Maa, Swami Nirvedananda ji and others, to compose scripts of plays in the same manner.

Some of the noted plays were: 'Tulsi Das', 'Naam Dev', 'Madhusudan Dada' etc. These plays used to be enacted regularly at Suri and other Ashrams, as part of the festive calendar and on other occasions as well.

These plays had several distinguishing features. First and foremost, these were based on devotion to God. Second, they were often used to be enacted on the spur of the moment, without any kind of rehearsal whatsoever. Third, often little children used to be the main actors in such plays.

For example, under the instructions of Sri Thakur, plays used to be often enacted extempore on open grounds. Here small children used to act, sing as well as dance. And each of them used to be given full freedom by Sri Thakur to make the use of his inborn talent to compose all the dialogues then and there and enact the best he could.

This used to be Sri Thakur's tried and tested method for arousing the creative potential, granted by God, to each child, so that latter can make continual progress in achieving the God-given Mission of his life. This was a wonderful prescription for the flowering of the innate Divinity of a child.

And the marvellous way small children and the monastic disciples used to act in these plays used to attract applause from everyone. The audience used to wonder how such amateur actors could play their individual roles so brilliantly. And it is a fact that the standard of acting by these amateur actors in some of these plays used to be so high that, in the opinion of learned people, such levels of excellence could be favourably compared to the best of professional actors in the theatre stages of Kolkata!

And, last but not the least, we need to make note of the fact that Sanskrit drama also used to be staged at Baranagar Ashram - this truly shared showed the respect of Sri Thakur towards the Divine language of Sanskrit.

In this manner, the seeds of Spirituality used to get spread far and wide through the novel medium of devotion-soaked plays of Ashram.

"Always repeat the Holy Name of God." - Sri Thakur

3. Dance

Divine culture expresses itself through various avenues such as music, theatre, painting, sculpture, and so on. In this sequence, dance was another creative medium, wonderfully utilized by Sri Thakur for strengthening the roots of devotion to God.

For this noble mission, informal sessions used to be regularly held in the Ashram compound, where small children (with no previous training) used to present extempore recitals of dance in sync with devotional music. And, these little dancers used to even present different 'mudra' (specific steps of dance), composed on the spot! Initially feeling shy, the children used to start dancing freely later on! All this wonder used to be made possible through the Grace of Sri Thakur!

And Sri Thakur also composed several dance dramas, whose main theme was devotion to God. The first such dance drama, written in Bengali, was "Borsha Baran" (Welcoming Monsoon) - Sri Thakur got it enacted by the children of devotees along with the students of a local School. And as per his custom, he did not engage any dance teacher and inspired the children to learn on their own under the informal guidance of their elders.

For dance recitals on special occasions (such as festive programs), he used to entrust Sanyasini mother Sharana Maa with the responsibility of guiding the dances of the participating children during rehearsals. And she used to fulfil that responsibility with total sincerity.

At times, during such rehearsals, Sri Thakur himself used to suggest improvement in the dancing steps of the participants. He could do so easily because of his inborn sense of artistic refinement. And, when such devotion-soaked dance recitals used to be finally presented on stage, the audience used to get moved by the strong vibrations of Spirituality!

The medium of dance was thus uniquely employed by Sri Thakur to encourage talent development among children on one hand and spread the message of Spirituality among the masses on the other hand.

"Ensure that you always keep repeating Holy Name of God within your mind." - Sri Thakur

CHAPTER TWELVE

Encouraging Learning and Wisdom

Sri Thakur is a role model to all of us because of his quest to learn all through his Divine life. This quest used to be evident in his love for interacting with scholars in various disciplines of learning - these experts used to keep on coming to the Ashram, pulled in by the magnetic aura of the God-Incarnate. They included both Indians as well as foreign scholars. While their informal meetings with Sri Thakur used to take place throughout the year, conferences of such scholars used to be specially arranged at the time of important festivals at Ashrams.

Now, let us look at some of the interesting titbits of these events:

1. Conferences of Indian Scholars

In the annual 'Sudhi Sammelan' held at Ashram, scholars - poets, authors, philosophers, professors and many other learned people used to be regularly invited. Sri Kumud Ranjan Mallick, Sri Naren Deb etc. were notable figures from the domain of Literature, while Dr Satish Chattopadhyay, Dr Mahendra Nath Sarkar etc. were some of the stalwart Philosophers. Mention must also be made of the renowned historian, Dr R C Majumdar who came over several times.

Sri Thakur, with an abiding faith in our rich heritage of Sanskrit language, also used to love meeting Sanskrit scholars such as Dr Gouri Nath Shastry, Dr Rama Chowdhury, and others, who used to regularly come to Ashram, attracted by the wonderful aura of Sri Thakur.

To illustrate the high quality of discussions at these scholars' conferences, we can refer to an actual session that occurred as a part of the celebration of the birth anniversary of Holy Mother, Maa Sarada in 1955. In that session, an eminent scholar had given a wonderful analogy to bring out the difference between Sri Ramakrishna Dev and Maa Sarada, in respect of granting the sacred 'Mantra Deeksha' to their devotees.

This learned scholar had pointed out that Sri Ramakrishna Dev resembled Professor Shambhu Bandopadhyay, a very strict professor who did not allow any student to pass the exam unless he had worked really hard to perform well in that paper.

On the other hand, Maa Sarada was like Professor Ashu Mukhopadhyay, a very lenient examiner, who used to allow a large number of students to easily pass the exam, irrespective of the level of their individual performance in his paper.

This was a very apt analogy as Sri Ramakrishna Dev was extremely choosy in the matter of selection of His disciples and granting them the holy spiritual initiation; on the other hand, Maa Sarada was very liberal in granting it to anyone approaching Her. On hearing such a beautiful comparison, the whole audience erupted with joy. And Sri Thakur, seated on the wings of the stage, also appreciated such high-quality thinking.

In this manner, under Sri Thakur's patronage, these annual conferences of scholars used to add immense value to the diversity of thoughts in spirituality and religion. In the hindsight, one can confidently assert that participants in those sessions were lucky indeed!

2. Meetings with Foreign Scholars

Foreign scholars used to regularly visit Sri Thakur's Ashram on various occasions. Examples included American Professors - Dr Smith and Dr James Whitehurst, French philosophers - Sylvain levy, Japanese Professor - J G Oshara and several other scholarly figures.

In fact, Dr Smith, after meeting Sri Thakur at Suri Ashram, stayed on for nearly one month there. And during this period, he used to enthusiastically participate in the holy rituals of Ashram such as Homa, Arati etc. He used to do so in compliance with the valuable advice of Sri Thakur, "Look Smith, you will have to know about the Spirituality of India in order to understand the pulse of India and to understand the Spirituality of India, you will have to voluntarily adopt a life of hardships." That is why he used to love accompanying Sri Thakur in going to 'Raas Ban', an Ashram located in between the banks of two rivers. And there, he used to merrily spend nights lying on an improvised bed made up of hay!

We can also mention about two other Americans, Levy and Cruise, who wanted to learn about the essence of Indian philosophy. That is why they chose to come to Suri Ashram and directly learn from Sri Thakur about the intricacies of different schools of thought in Indian philosophy. They also willingly opted for a life of austerity in order to quench their thirst for knowledge. And deeply enriched with their learning at the lotus feet of Sri Thakur, they went back to their parent country happily.

"To be virtuous requires 'a strong will to be good' as its foundation." - Sri Thakur

3. Shishu Sammelan

Sri Thakur's earnest effort was to spread Divinity among all strata of the population. That is why the children, the future of our country, were always included among the audience of his spiritual endeavours.

In this sequence, a unique cultural event called 'Shishu Sammelan' used to be regularly organized at the Ashrams as a part of the annual festive calendar. In these events, only children could take part as the participants and as the audience. Here, the child artists used to present a wonderful bouquet of cultural programs comprising recitation, singing, dancing and other items to the audience.

And as a novel gesture, the Chairman of these events used to be a child always! This unique practice used to be followed, even when renowned writers of children's fiction such as Mr Bimal Ghosh, Mr Prabhat K Basu etc. used to grace these programs, as the Chief Guest on special invitation.

Truly the way these conferences were organized used to be unique in all respects! Such events used to go a long way towards the spread of Divine culture among the tiny tots, the citizens of our country tomorrow.

"God dwells in each of our hearts. Go on praying to Him. He will cause your mind to get focused towards Divinity." - Sri Thakur

CHAPTER THIRTEEN

Supporting the Cause of Honest Livelihood

Sri Thakur always upheld the principle, "work is worship". That's why he used to encourage his renunciate disciples (the Sanyasis and the Sanyasini mothers) to acquire higher educational qualifications and serve as Teachers in the schools run under the aegis of his Ashrams.

Encouraged by him, quite a few of them went on to earn BA, MA and even PhD degrees and then, serve as Teachers in Schools and Colleges set up by Sri Thakur. As he used to rightly emphasise, they could earn their living independently that way and thus, avoid depending on anyone for meeting their needs.

And He used to always encourage his householder disciples to work sincerely in their chosen vocations such as service, business etc. and earn their livelihood by honest means. He was fully sympathetic towards their lot as he knew they were carrying a huge financial burden on their shoulders in this age of relentless price-rise and competition. But, at the same time, he also used to emphasise to them the need to cultivate the virtue of contentment and joyfully accept whatever one earns as the Blessings of God.

In the same vein, he always used to motivate the students of his schools to study hard, acquire high qualifications and get good jobs in order to earn well and take care of their parents, on one hand, and contribute to the economic welfare of the country, the other hand.

And last but not the least, he always used to inspire everyone to contribute a part of his earnings towards charity for the upkeep of Religious Institutions such as Ashrams and Temples. That's because, as Sri Thakur used to rightly say, we can earn our living only because of the Grace of God.

This, in a nutshell, is the gist of Sri Thakur's outlook on the economic necessity of earning a livelihood.

"The hallmark of Divinity is a disciplined life." - Sri Thakur

CHAPTER FOURTEEN

Legacy of Sri Thakur

Sri Thakur was a Divine genius, who left his indelible mark, on each area of life touched by him.

These encompass a very broad range of domains such as religion, spirituality, art, culture, education, training, philanthropy, social reforms, economic livelihood, and so on.

While we have already seen his unique contributions in these areas, here is a recap for our easy reference:

1. Puja:

It is often said that Sarada Devi (consort of Bhagavan Sri Ramakrishna Dev) is the Mother Goddess Herself. But to demonstrate this in-ground reality is in a completely different league altogether.

And Sri Thakur did so through the unique ceremony of 'Sarada-Durga Puja' held annually at his Baranagar Ashram. Even now, this is probably the only place, where Sarada Devi is worshipped as Goddess Durga.

2. Ashram:

A mighty oak lies hidden in a tiny acorn. In the same manner, the Suri Ashram, which started in a small manner with just a handful of devotees in 1939, gave rise to branch Ashrams at so many locations in Bengal as well as Bihar, within quite a short period.

3. Leela of Sri Gopal ji:

Sri Thakur was the Incarnation of Bhagavan Sri Narayan, one of whose forms is Gopal ji. Hence, the unique Leela of Sri Gopal ji was, in effect, the unique Leela of Sri Thakur Himself.

4. Daily Spiritual Discourse:

The way Sri Thakur used to unify spirituality and science during his daily discourses at the Ashrams is truly unparalleled in the chronicles of spiritual tradition in India!

5. United Nations Organization of Hinduism:

This was another novel contribution of Sri Thakur in conceptual form. If this idea gets implemented in its true spirit, then it will bring in the much-desired unity among different sects of Hinduism.

6. Education:

Sri Thakur always emphasized that the God-given talent of a child can flower to its fullest potential if virtuous means are adopted during that unfolding process and if worship of God is its ultimate aim. This was one of his great contributions toward the worthy cause of man-making education.

7. Compassion and Love for Humanity:

Sri Thakur showed a unique path for the uplifting of the so-called low-caste 'untouchables' of our society through granting the sacred 'Sanyas Deeksha' to the spiritually deserving individuals among them.

8. Divine Art and Culture:

Here the unique contribution of Sri Thakur lay in the use of non-conventional means like drama for spreading spiritual vibrations among the masses.

9. Shishu Sammelan:

This was Sri Thakur's beautiful method for arousing the latent potential for excellence, granted by God, to each child. That's why he conceived of the unique idea of having a small child to be the Chairman of these conferences, where literary figures (as reputed as Sri Prabhat Kiran Basu and others) used to be invited to be the Chief Guests.

10. Adoption of Monastic life by Entire Families:

Finally, we would like to make a special mention of Sri Thakur's novel contribution: the adoption of monastic life by entire families under his Divine inspiration!

Here, let me try to paint a picture of what usually happens when an individual decides to adopt a life of Spirituality. Realising the futility of this material life, he starts developing an urge towards a life of renunciation. As a result, he decides to leave his household and go to a suitable Guru. After carrying out austerities under Guru's guidance for a prolonged period, he makes progress in his chosen path. And, he gets blessed with the sacred vows of 'Brahmacharya' and later on, 'Sanyas' in due course of time.

But his other family members remain unaffected: initially they try to actively dissuade him and failing that, they continue their worldly life as usual. They remain sceptical about Spirituality and at times, they even display open hostility towards it.

Under the Divine influence of Sri Thakur, however, something radically different began to occur! And this was the unprecedented event of whole families taking shelter under Sri Thakur and then adopting the life of renunciation!

Normally, one member of a family, after meeting Sri Thakur at his Ashram, used to feel deeply attracted to the life of spirituality, and then, later on, join the Ashram fraternity. But soon the magnetic attraction of Sri Thakur used to cast its irreversible spell over the rest of the family as well. And lo and behold! The new Monk's father, mother, siblings - everyone used to gladly surrender themselves at the lotus feet of Sri Thakur and become monks too!

There are so many examples to illustrate this unparalleled magic of Sri Thakur. Just as an example, we can quote the name of Sri Satinath, a middle-class householder, who initially adopted the life of celibacy under Sri Thakur's encouragement, and in due course, the rest of his family comprising his wife and three sons adopted the monastic path as well.

We can also cite the example of three sisters of the town of Suri joining Sri Thakur's Ashram and receiving vows of 'Brahmacharya' and later on, 'Sanyas'. They were the Sanyasini Mothers: Sharana Maa, Arati Maa and Aradhana Maa.

And the most appropriate examples would be that of the adoption of Spiritual life by respected Sanyasini Archana Maa and her father in pre monastic life, Swami Nirvedananda ji - both of whom were counted among the foremost disciples of Sri Thakur.

The above examples are just samples and serve to illustrate the magnificent Spiritual aura of Sri Thakur.

"Always keep your mind attuned towards the Higher Plane - be it in the spiritual matter or be it in the worldly affair." - Sri Thakur

CHAPTER FIFTEEN

Sri Thakur's Guidance for Life in the 21st Century

Friends, now that we are nearing the end of this account, let us ask ourselves: What have we learnt? What are our takeaways? And most importantly, how can we apply such learning in our day-to-day life?

All the above questions become supremely relevant as we grapple with life in the 21st century where daily complexities and challenges have increased beyond imagination. Just one example is the advent of the ubiquitous smartphone.

So let us attempt finding the answers by praying for the guidance of Sri Thakur, whose very life was his teaching.

First and foremost, Sri Thakur used to lay the highest stress on constantly repeating the Holy Name of God. His golden advice was to repeat the Holy Name of God with every single in-breath and out-breath.

So dear friends, let us adopt this honourable way of living - this will help us remain connected with God in a 24/7 manner in our life. It's quite possible that many times we'll falter as we start this new habit - many times, we'll forget to repeat the Holy Name of God - many times, we'll go back to our old sensuous way of living. But all these things do not matter in the least. The moment we remember that we have stopped repeating the Holy Name of God, the very next moment we can resume. Trust me, this one single effort is going to bring in the most magical transformation in life!

Second, Sri Thakur used to lay the greatest stress on cultivating the companionship of the holy for moral purity in day-to-day life. Friends, right now, all of us possess a smartphone; many of us own more than one. Let us start using them for bringing in the welcome rays of goodness into our lives. We can start by using our smartphones to regularly visit the websites of Religious and Spiritual Institutions: this virtuous habit will cause blessings of God to get showered on our life. This is because 'God is good and good is God' and hence, consciously choosing the path of goodness will lead us to God.

Most importantly, Sri Thakur has done a yeomen service to humanity at large by abolishing all the conventional differences between the Spiritual life and the so-called secular life. This implies that besides the accepted paths of worshipping God such as Puja, Japa, Dhyana, and reading Scriptures, the mundane activities of our day-to-day lives such as work at offices and homes are equally acceptable means as well!

So, let us worship God by any path that suits our lifestyle - our lives will get blessed many times over.

"Keep on persevering towards your goal with strong faith." - Sri Thakur

CHAPTER SIXTEEN

A Humble Submission

Friends, with the grace of Sri Thakur, we have tried to offer homage to him by painting this short sketch of his illustrious life in words. This is just like the way we pay our homage to Mother Ganga by offering her waters to herself.

However, as already stated at the very beginning of this volume, full justice can hardly be done to the Infinite expanse of his Godly life in such a brief account. So, all that has been attempted is touching only upon the salient points.

After going through this humble narrative, if you are inspired to know more about the sacred life of Sri Thakur, I'll consider my modest effort to have partially met its aim. You can do so by visiting the comprehensive website: *sreesatyanandamahapeeth.com.* And you are also welcome to visit any of the Ashrams of Sri Thakur. The addresses of the main Ashrams in Kolkata are:

i) Sri Ramakrishna Ashram,
1, Pran Krishna Saha Lane, Baranagar,
Kolkata - 700036

ii)Sree Satyananda Devayatan
1, Ibrahimpur Road, Jadavpur,
Kolkata - 700032

It is well said that an ounce of practice is worth a thousand words. Hence, the ultimate effectiveness of reading this account will rest in moulding our own lives as per the golden standards of Sri Thakur's Saintly life. That is why, as we go through this account, it is imperative that we simultaneously reflect on its inner significance so that we gain the righteous direction for our lives.

Thereafter, through earnest prayers to Sri Thakur, we can start bringing in positive changes in our lives in a gradual manner. How much we are thus able to elevate ourselves is less important. What truly matters is that we begin to move on the right path.

And this is because, as aptly uttered by Bhagavan Ramakrishna Dev, as we start moving towards the Holy town of Kashi (representing virtues), the worldly town of Kolkata (the stronghold of vice) will automatically start receding further and further away from us.

With these words, I hereby place my modest offering at the lotus feet of Sri Thakur and pray for his compassionate love and ever-present Grace to bless our lives.

"Jai Maa"

Prayers

Maa,

We offer our homage to Your lotus feet! Only due to Your Infinite Grace, this humble account could be written! Please have mercy and forgive all the mistakes made here. May this account help us in finding the righteous direction for our lives.

"Jai Maa"

Printed by Libri Plureos GmbH in Hamburg,
Germany